THIS IS AN URGENT MESSAGE FROM A VISITOR TO YOUR PLANET

By Ruomyes Snassel

This Is An Urgent Message From A Visitor To Your Planet

Ruomyes Snassel

Published by Safeworld Publishing Company, 2020.

Printed in the United States of America

ISBN: 978-0-9655604-7-4 (EPUB)

ISBN: 978-1-954284-88-3 (Paperback)

ISBN: 978-1-954284-24-1 (Adobe PDF)

Safeworld Publishing Company

Table of Contents

FOR THE BENEFIT OF ALL MANKIND

PROLOGUE

Our VISITOR reveals, in the first few pages, the reason their GREAT TRANSITION was delayed 500 years, and a similar thing could happen here because we have also been taught to believe, through words that do not symbolize reality but give the appearance of doing so, that a certain aspect of man's nature is absolutely true. As a consequence, the natural, psychological law, hidden behind the door stating that this "aspect of man's nature" is false, could remain permanently concealed because our leading authorities, the very people who don't know the truth but think they do, may never desire to open that door for a thorough investigation when the claim of what can be accomplished appears ridiculous, impossible, and compromises the integrity of their knowledge and capability. If they can't solve our problems, and they are the experts, it stands to reason that no one else can. However, if you will bear in mind how many times in the course of history has the IMPOSSIBLE (that which appeared to be) been made possible by a scientific breakthrough, you will refrain from jumping to a premature conclusion, will give this VISITOR the benefit of the doubt, will open that hermetically sealed door in spite of appearances, and then, after a complete study of all the principles involved, will be able to see that our NEW WORLD must become a reality sooner or later and could take place within the 21st century, if this natural law is released from its hiding place quickly enough and thoroughly understood.

By revealing this law to mankind for the very first time, he is given no choice in this matter whatsoever, although when this change in human conduct occurs will depend on when scientists confirm it with the brevet of truth. We have been growing and developing just like a child from infancy. There is no way a baby can go from birth to old age without passing through the necessary steps of baby teeth, puberty, etc., and no way man could have reached this tremendous turning point in his life without first going through the necessary stages of evil. The only thing required now to deliver our planet from the many forms of hurt plaguing human relations is to open our minds and refrain from jumping to the conclusion that we already know the truth about man's ultimate nature. However, to fully understand the principles and the significance of this knowledge, it is necessary to study this book chapter by chapter (no skipping). The first 5 chapters are absolutely essential because this natural law is then extended into every human relation. Please understand that any truth revealed in an undeniable manner does not require our approval for its validity, although it does necessitate our understanding for recognition and development. And now my friends, let us welcome our visitor and heed his words... for the hour is getting late.

THE MESSAGE IS THIS

S hortly after my arrival I was so completely taken aback by what exists here, that at first I found it difficult to believe, until the reason was made apparent by the realization that your scientists never discovered the natural, psychological law of man's ultimate nature, which, over 50,000 years ago, brought about on our globe what we refer to as THE GREAT TRANSITION. We have no war or crime and do nothing to hurt each other because this law prevents us from striking the first blow; and this eliminates the need to blame, punish, to retaliate or to turn the other cheek.

The reason we were able to make this discovery that still lies beyond the framework of your thought, is because life began on our planet long before it did on yours, and as a consequence our mental development, our ability to perceive difficult but undeniable relations, is more advanced. To test this I asked several professors to arrange 10 alphabetical blocks divided equally between A and O in groups of 3 and in 7 lines, so that no letter is ever twice with the same letter. Five gave up in one month. Three said it could not be done. The remaining two revealed by their answer that they never even understood the question which is worked out by our 13-year-old children. This in itself doesn't mean that you will be incapable of comprehending this law, but it certainly points in that direction because your thinkers also stand today regarding the nature of man, where your ancestors stood when they believed the Earth flat. Until accurate thinking scientists exploded this realistic but fallacious theory by discovering the true shape of your planet, the invariable laws revealing the mathematical harmony of your solar system and giving you the knowledge to predict an eclipse and land men on the moon, remained undiscovered.

This natural law is your long sought "OUNCE OF PREVENTION," your long-awaited MESSIAH, the BREAKTHROUGH you could never find. But I would like to point out that even though this law is completely undeniable (three is to six what four is to eight), it still required nearly 500 years before we were able to launch our New World. The reason for this became a classic that was recorded in Adnil's autobiography. I can almost remember it word for word. In fact, he became so excited after discovering this law that he immediately contacted a group of leading authorities to tell them about it and was granted an audience. The interview went as follows:

"Mr. Adnil, you told us when we were first contacted that you made a fantastic discovery that will put a permanent end to war and crime, and you were invited here because we would like to learn how such a miracle can be accomplished. But your claim not only sounds impossible but somewhat ridiculous in view of man's nature. We don't mind listening if it won't take too long. We do have another engagement but can devote at least one hour, so please be as brief as possible. By the way, from what university did you graduate, and what was your specialty?"

THIS IS AN URGENT MESSAGE FROM A VISITOR TO YOUR PLANET

"I sincerely hope that my educational background is of no significance here, because I dropped out of school at the age of thirteen, but I did a lot of reading and studying on my own."

"Of course it doesn't, Mr. Adnil, so go right ahead."

"I will try to accommodate you by being brief as possible, but in order to reveal my discovery it is absolutely necessary that I first show you its hiding place because they are related to each other. You see, Gentlemen, most people believe, consciously or unconsciously, that man's will is free . . ."

"What's that?" exclaimed their leader rather vehemently. "Did I hear you correctly? Are you trying to tell us that the will of man is not free?"

"That is absolutely true, sir, and my discovery lies locked behind the door marked MAN'S WILL IS NOT FREE, just like the laws of our solar system were concealed because we believed our planet was flat — until some upstart scientist discovered the truth."

"But the door of determinism was opened many times through the years, and the principles studied by some of the most profound thinkers, and never did they come up with any discoveries to change the world. If you had studied at any of our universities, you would have known this."

"It is true, I agree, that determinism was investigated by some of the most profound thinkers, but in spite of their profoundness, none of them had the capacity to perceive the law that was hidden there."

"I don't know what it is you think you discovered, Mr. Adnil, but whatever it is, it cannot be valid and therefore must be a fraud because we know for a fact, and I speak for every person here, that man's will is definitely free beyond any doubts. Thank you very much for coming out, but we are not interested in discussing this matter further."

Adnil eventually received posthumous recognition when a group of special investigators with an established reputation for wisdom and knowledge stumbled upon his work and after months of serious analysis, publicly confirmed his natural law.

There were many books written on the subject after that, but now all of us not only understand but live by this law because we are given NO CHOICE to do otherwise. This does not mean, as some of you might think, that we are forced, against our will, to "live by this law"; it only means that when confronted with the choice of hurting or not hurting others with a FIRST BLOW, we are compelled to choose the latter because the former, under the changed conditions imposed by this law, is an impossible consideration. How many times in your life have you said, or heard it said, "You give me NO CHOICE?" Well, believe it or not, and this will be undeniably proven, your CREATOR, (please note that my use of the word 'Creator' is not the focus of this message, yet it could give rise to arguments over the existence of God. This would be an unnecessary distraction and take away from the purpose for my visit) by the revelation of these NATURAL LAWS, is giving you NO CHOICE in this matter whatsoever by showing you the way to deliver yourselves from evil. However, I'm not an author, teacher, scientist, or professional of any kind, just an ordinary individual, so bear with me as I attempt to condense many thousands of pages and innumerable books into a small book capable of being understood. Therefore, without further ado, and because my time here is very limited, I shall begin.

THIS IS AN URGENT MESSAGE FROM A VISITOR TO YOUR PLANET

PART ONE

Your skepticism at this point is normal, but your smile of incredulity will be wiped from your face once you begin to study the text <u>chapter by chapter</u>, of which the first three are most fundamental.

CHAPTER ONE — THE GREAT IMPASSE

CHAPTER TWO — THE TWO-SIDED EQUATION

CHAPTER THREE — CARELESSNESS

CHAPTER ONE
THE GREAT IMPASSE

Your belief in free will came into existence out of absolute necessity, not only so theology could relieve God of all responsibility for evil, but primarily because it was impossible not to blame and punish the people obviously responsible for committing these terrible crimes, which required the justification of this belief in order to absolve your conscience. In other words, if you were called upon to pass judgment on someone by sentencing him to death for murder, could you do it with a clear conscience if you knew, for an absolute fact, that his will was not free, that he was compelled to that act by laws over which he had no control? To punish him in any way, you would have to believe that he was free to choose another alternative than the one for which he was convicted, that he was not compelled to this act by laws over which he had no control. You were given no choice but to think this way, and that is why you developed the principle of an "EYE FOR AN EYE AND A TOOTH FOR A TOOTH" and why this natural law was never discovered on your planet and delayed for a long time from coming to light on ours. No one could ever get beyond this point because if man's will is not free, it becomes absolutely impossible to hold you responsible no matter what you choose to do. Well, is it any wonder this natural law was never found if it lies beyond that point? How is it possible not to blame people for murder, rape, and the slaughter of millions? The belief that man's will is not free strikes at the very heart of your civilization. Right at this point lies the crux of a problem so difficult of solution that it has prevented you from discovering this natural law that has the amazing power of delivering your planet from evil. Therefore, it is necessary that I proceed in a step-by-step process that brooks no opposition because you will be unable to deny what is being demonstrated, and I shall begin by proving that what you do of your own free will, of your own desire because you want to, is done absolutely and positively not of your own free will. This will not remove the GREAT IMPASSE or reveal the natural law, but it is the first step.

In reality, you are carried along on the wings of time or life during every moment of your existence, and have no say in this matter whatsoever. You cannot stop yourself from being born and are compelled to live out your life the best you can. Is it possible to disagree with this? But since it is absolutely impossible to be both dead and alive at the same time, and since it is absolutely impossible to desire suicide unless dissatisfied with life (regardless of the reason), you are given the ability to demonstrate a revealing and undeniable relation.

You are now standing on the present moment of time called here, and are given two alternatives. Either live by moving to the next moment of time called there or remain here where you are by committing suicide. If you are still reading, then it is obvious that you are not satisfied to remain here by committing suicide and prefer moving to the next moment of time called <u>there</u>. Consequently, the motion of life, which is any motion from <u>here</u> to <u>there</u>, is a movement away from that which dissatisfies, otherwise, had you been satisfied to remain <u>here</u> where you are, you would never have moved to there. Since the motion of life constantly moves from <u>here</u> to <u>there</u>, which is an expression of dissatisfaction with the present position or <u>here</u>, you are under a compulsion, from the day of your birth to the day of your death, to move in the direction of what gives you greater satisfaction. But let me elaborate on this a little.

The reason you sometimes get confused over freedom of the will is because the word choice is very misleading for it assumes that you have two or more alternatives, but in reality this is a delusion because the direction of life, always moving towards greater satisfaction, compels you to prefer of differences what you consider better for yourself, and when two or more alternatives are presented, you are compelled, by your very nature, to prefer not that one which you consider the worse of the two, but what gives every indication of being better for the particular set of circumstances involved. You may immediately regret your choice and say you made a mistake, but at that moment of time, you chose the one alternative that gave you greater satisfaction.

The purpose of choosing between A and B is to compare meaningful differences to decide which is preferable. The difference considered favorable, regardless of the reason, is the compulsion or greater satisfaction desire is forced to take, which makes one of them an impossible choice because it gives you less satisfaction. Therefore, since B is an impossible choice, you are not free to choose A. You can cite hundreds of examples to prove that man's will is not free, but there is no need to go any further in that direction. However, and here again is where you get confused. Even though you are compelled to choose the alternative that gives you greater satisfaction, nothing in this world can make you do anything against your will, or anything you don't want to do, for over this, your nature gives you absolute control. This simply means that if you were to say that you were compelled to do what you did against your will, that you really didn't want to but had to because you were being tortured, you are obviously confused and unconsciously lying to others and yourself because you could die before being forced to do something against your will. What you actually mean is that you didn't like being tortured because the pain was unbearable, so instead of continuing to suffer this way, you preferred, as the lesser of two evils, to tell your captors what they wanted to know, but you did this because you wanted to, not because they made you do this against your will. If, by talking, you knew that someone you were in love with would be instantly killed, death might have been judged the lesser of two evils and given you greater satisfaction.

This is an extremely crucial point because, though will is not free, absolutely nothing on this earth can make you do anything against your will. To repeat, you might not like some of the things you choose to do, but you wanted to do them because the alternative, at that moment of time, gave you no free or better choice.

And now I shall demonstrate how these two undeniable laws or principles — that nothing can compel you to do anything against your will because, over this, your nature allows absolute control, and that your will is not free because your nature also

THIS IS AN URGENT MESSAGE FROM A VISITOR TO YOUR PLANET

compels you to prefer of alternatives the one that offers greater satisfaction — will reveal the natural law that will bring about your GREAT TRANSITION.

RUOMYES SNASSEL

CHAPTER TWO
THE TWO-SIDED EQUATION

O nce it is established as an undeniable law that the will of man is not free, as was just demonstrated, you can no longer assume it is free because your leading authorities cannot get by the implications of determinism. Therefore, you must begin your reasoning where they left off, which means that you are going to accept the corollary, THOU SHALL NOT BLAME, even though it presents what appears to be insurmountable, for how is it possible not to blame people who hurt you when you know they didn't have to do this if they didn't want to? Let me show you how this apparent impasse can be rephrased in terms of possibility.

If you are not being hurt in any way, is it possible to retaliate or to turn the other cheek? Isn't it obvious that in order to do either, you must first be hurt? But if you are being hurt and by turning the other cheek you make matters worse for yourself, then you are given no choice but to retaliate because this is demanded by your nature, which compels you to prefer the alternative that gives you greater satisfaction. Here is the source of the confusion. The basic principle or corollary, THOU

SHALL NOT BLAME (call it what you will), is not going to accomplish the impossible. It is not going to prevent you from wanting to hurt others when not doing so makes matters worse for yourself, but it will prevent your desire to strike the very first blow. If you are wondering what would prevent you from satisfying your desires to your heart's content when you know there will be no more consequences, has it been forgotten already that you are compelled, by your nature, to choose the alternative that gives you greater satisfaction, which is the reason your will is not free? Consequently, to solve this problem it is only necessary to demonstrate that when all blame is removed from the environment and when the conditions are also removed that make it necessary for you to hurt others because not to do so makes matters worse for yourself, the desire to hurt them will be the worst possible choice. In other words, the knowledge that there will be no consequences presents consequences that are still worse, making it impossible to consider this hurt as a preferable alternative. If will were free, you could not accomplish this because you would be able to choose what is worse for yourself when something better is available, but this natural law of your nature, soon to be revealed, will give you no alternative when you are forced to obey it in order to derive greater satisfaction. Let me show you what I mean.

At this moment of time in your world of free will you are trying to decide whether to hurt others in some way, but you had everything removed that could be used to justify this act. You simply see an opportunity to gain some advantage at their expense, but should you decide against it, you will not be a loser, that is, you will not make matters worse for yourself. In other words, you are contemplating the very first blow.

THIS IS AN URGENT MESSAGE FROM A VISITOR TO YOUR PLANET

You realize there is a certain risk involved, if caught, because you must face the consequences. But if what you are planning to do is not that serious, you may be able to get away with it by offering all kinds of reasonable excuses as to why you had no choice. To ridicule determinism and unwittingly reveal your confusion, you might try to shift your responsibility by saying, "I could not help myself because man's will is not free." But if there is no way any excuse is acceptable, as in a court of law after you have been found guilty, and there is no other way to satisfy your desires unless the risk is taken, you are prepared to pay a price for the crime of hurting others with a first blow.

Under these conditions it is impossible for your conscience to exercise any control over your desires, because you can't feel any guilt just as long as you are prepared to suffer the consequences. But observe what miracle happens when the two laws clearly discussed in the first chapter, and mentioned again in its last paragraph, are brought together to reveal the natural law to which reference has been made several times.

For the very first time, you know as a matter of undeniable knowledge that absolutely nothing in this world, that no one can compel you to do anything against your will, for over this you know you have absolute control. Not only does this prevent you from shifting your responsibility, but how is it possible to blame other people or other things for what you know you have done when no one on your planet blames you? It cannot be done. This does not mean that other people and other things are not often responsible for the hurt that is done as part of a chain reaction, as when an employer is forced to lay off his employees because the money to pay them has stopped coming in to him, but no one is blaming him for what is obviously not his responsibility, and therefore it isn't necessary for him to offer excuses.

Now here you are contemplating this hurt (doing to others what they don't want done to themselves), while they know as a matter of positive knowledge that you cannot be blamed anymore because it is an undeniable law that man's will is not free. This is a very unique two-sided equation, for it reveals that while you know you are completely responsible for everything you choose to do to hurt others, they know you can no longer be held responsible. For the very first time, you fully realize that they must excuse you because it is an undeniable law that man must always select of available alternatives the one that offers greater satisfaction. This prevents you from thinking of excuses in advance because you know you are already excused. Should you go ahead with this first blow, you can't apologize or ask forgiveness because you are already forgiven, and no one is blaming you. This means that should you decide to hurt others with this first blow or be careless and take the risks that lead to a first blow, and they would have to choose between retaliating or turning the other cheek, you would know that they would be compelled to find greater satisfaction in turning the other cheek because of the undeniable fact that they would know you had no choice to do otherwise. But remember (and here is the solution so pay close attention), you haven't hurt them yet because this is still under consideration, and when it fully dawns on you, this hurt to them will not be questioned, judged, or blamed in any way because they don't want to hurt you for doing what must now be considered a compulsion beyond your control, ALTHOUGH YOU KNOW IT IS NOT BEYOND YOUR CONTROL at this point since nothing can force you to hurt them unless you want to, you are compelled to relinquish this contemplated hurt because you will never be able to derive greater satisfaction under the changed conditions. In other words, it becomes the worst possible alternative to take advantage of not being blamed, because there is no advantage in hurting those whom you know must excuse what you can no longer justify. CONSCIENCE (which in your present world lies between one and three on a scale of ten), your GUILTY FEELING over such an act will not permit it because you will get less satisfaction, not more.

It should be obvious that as long as you are able to justify hurting others, which can only be done when not hurting them makes matters worse for yourself, you are not striking a first blow. But before I demonstrate how this last vestige of justification is permanently removed and to allow you an opportunity to see exactly what happens in a human relationship where it is already removed, I shall perform a virtual miracle in the next chapter by revealing how all automobile accidents must come to a permanent end.

RUOMYES SNASSEL

CHAPTER THREE
CARELESSNESS

To understand how this will be accomplished, I shall show you exactly what takes place in your present environment before and after a collision, although you already know and have experienced this, and then let you see the same accident under the changed conditions.

Actually, the only reason you are willing to "Drive Carefully" and take no risks is "because the life you save may be your own." This allows you to be careless because there are many ways you can shift your responsibility (remember, you are innocent until proven guilty), and you carry liability insurance to help you pay for damages just in case you are found guilty. But when it becomes impossible to shift our responsibility or pay a price, you are forced to do everything in your power to prevent a careless hurt because it is the only alternative that will give you greater satisfaction. Take note.

Not so long ago, a truck was heading west inside the city limits, doing 50 miles an hour in a 25-mile zone. It was past midnight, and very few cars were on the street. The driver was anxious to get home because he hadn't seen his family for two weeks. He had driven this route many times and knew it was safe to go at that speed at that time of the morning. His only concern was to keep an eye out for a patrol car so he would not get a ticket. Up ahead, four blocks away, he saw that a traffic light was green. When about one-half block away, he knew from experience that it would soon be joined with the yellow and followed, in a few seconds, with the red, indicating that he would have to stop. But since this was a nuisance, since the amber light had not yet gone on, and since the surrounding darkness enabled him to see that no lights were coming from other directions, he felt safe to increase his speed to 65 miles an hour. But heading north was a car carrying five people. A father, a mother, and their three children. They had just attended a wedding and were on their way home. The father had been drinking rather heavily and completely forgot to put on his headlights. He was also driving along at 50 miles an hour when he slowed down so he wouldn't have to stop for the red light up ahead, but when he saw the yellow light go on for the other direction, and judging that the light would be green before getting to the intersection even if he resumed his 50 miles an hour, he didn't hesitate to do just that. Now, just before the truck got to the crossing, the light changed, which meant that the truck driver would have to go through on the red, and at that very moment he saw the car, without any lights on, enter the intersection a second ahead of him, but it was too late to avoid the collision. The father saw the truck at that instant too. They both jammed on their brakes and turned their wheels instinctively, but the truck ploughed head on, at a slight angle, into the rear right side of the car, killing all three children.

If the truck driver had any inkling that such an accident would have resulted from his trying to beat the light, he certainly would never have taken the risk, but at that moment of time, because he was anxious to get home, he chose the alternative that gave him greater satisfaction. However, we are not interested now in what he should or should not have done, but only in what he must do for greater satisfaction following this accident. It is obvious he feels absolutely horrible over what he knows was his fault, but he doesn't want to be blamed for the death of these children. There is certainly no satisfaction in feeling the weight of this responsibility, so he is going to do everything in his power to shift it away from himself.

The police arrive and learn that the father was driving without lights on and that he was somewhat intoxicated. The truck driver kept saying over and over to the police, "This accident was definitely not my fault. That man went right through the red light and didn't even have his lights on. The death of these children is terrible, but it was not my fault." Before long, he was absolutely convinced that the accident would never have happened had the headlights been on, and he was probably right because what made him speed up was his certainty that no car was coming. But he could not tell the police the truth because the right of way still belonged to the father, even though intoxicated and without lights, but it made him feel so much better.

In court, the father was found guilty of manslaughter even though he was completely innocent, which infuriated him because he knew he had the right of way, but because the death of his children was considered punishment enough, his sentence was suspended, and he was placed on probation. His wife, however, was not satisfied with the verdict since she believed he was guilty of killing their children (she had warned him time and again about his heavy drinking at parties) and told him she wanted a divorce. The truck driver was awarded quite a bit of money in damages because he and his doctor claimed that he was not physically and mentally the same after such a traumatic experience. If he felt the least bit guilty over causing the death of these children and the breakup of their marriage, he could always confess this sin to his priest or psychiatrist or atone for it in various ways. The father, on the other hand, who was found guilty when completely innocent, builds up tremendous hatred for the whole system of justice because his life was ruined, and he wants to hurt somebody, anybody, in the worst way. Now pay close attention to the same accident under changed conditions.

The truck driver feels absolutely horrible over what he knows was his responsibility, but he also knows that no one in the entire world, not even the parents who lost their children, will ever blame him. How do you think he feels knowing also that he could have avoided that accident had he kept the same speed and stopped at the light? If only he could turn back the clock and undo what his carelessness did. Would it not be wonderful if he could find some way to shift his responsibility, or, at the very least, pay a price for what he did? He has no one to lie to. He can't even lie to himself. This means that he is compelled to go through life with the death of these children on his conscience. But let's examine this from another point of view.

Suppose the father didn't see the truck at all and wasn't certain of what happened. He might actually believe that his drinking was responsible, that maybe he did forget to put on his lights, that he did go through the red light, and how do you think he feels knowing that his drinking might have caused the death of his own children? How is it possible for you to know you are not responsible for such an accident unless you are fully aware at all times of what you're doing? This means that the thought of hurting others through pure carelessness is so terrifying to contemplate when there will be no blame or price to be paid for what you know is, or might have been, your responsibility, that when you are confronted with a similar situation as the truck driver, you could never find greater satisfaction in speeding up; and if you are at a party and know that drinking excessively might cause you to get in an accident, you will either limit what you drink or do not drive at all. And you will move in this direction not because you are forced to do it, but only because you will want to do it.

The right of way system will become a mathematical standard by which you are forced to judge only yourself should an accident occur, but carelessness is on its way out along with auto accidents. You can't afford to drive with bad tires or brakes because if one blows out and the other fails, forcing you to collide with other cars by entering their right of way, you have no one to blame when no one blames you. Even if you found out that it was not your fault because it was something in the road or the wheel came off because the bolts were carelessly tightened by your mechanic, who is blaming you or him? If you are concerned about any expenses to your car caused by the carelessness of others, you will be able to carry No Fault insurance if you feel the need. But don't get ahead of me and jump to conclusions about your economic world, which will be discussed shortly.

Before you will desire to drive a car, you will want to know everything that might make you responsible for an accident that will then not occur. You will also want to learn all the things you could possibly do to delay people from getting to their destination; and if by not using directional signals when required, or by not moving over far enough, you see that you are holding up traffic for which you are not being blamed by the blowing of horns, you will soon find greater satisfaction in not doing anything to hold up traffic. As for whether you need permission from your government to drive. . .

In your present environment you do because you are irresponsible. But in your new environment, your responsibility increases to its maximum degree, and you won't be too anxious to sit behind the wheel until you know you can drive without causing accidents or delays. This means that you won't have to prove to anyone but yourself that you are qualified to drive. Even driving instructors will never tell you when they think you are ready. This is your responsibility. However, to launch your GREAT TRANSITION and create the total environment necessary to prevent not only accidents but wars, crimes, and all the other evils plaguing your lives requires much more than these three chapters.

Your belief in free will and the concomitant blame are equivalent to the thrust of a rocket in getting a satellite into space, for without it, you could never have reached the outposts of this fantastic new world. But just as the astronauts shed their excess baggage when their rocket has expended its energy in reaching orbit, so likewise will you shed this theory and all the blame that helped you reach this tremendous turning point in your lives. Before I enter your economic world and perform another virtual miracle, I will reveal two other natural laws about your nature never understood.

THIS IS AN URGENT MESSAGE FROM A VISITOR TO YOUR PLANET

PART TWO

The chapters here have no relation to the first three, but they will change your life in an unbelievable manner.

CHAPTER FOUR — WORDS, NOT REALITY

CHAPTER FIVE — YOUR POSTERITY

RUOMYES SNASSEL

CHAPTER FOUR
WORDS, NOT REALITY

Just as the first natural law was not that man's will is not free but the two-sided equation which was hermetically sealed behind that door, so likewise, the natural law to be revealed in this chapter is not that MAN DOES NOT HAVE FIVE SENSES, but what significant knowledge lies hidden behind that door.

The word sense is defined as "any receptor, or group of receptors, specialized to receive and transmit external stimuli as of sight, taste, hearing, touch, and smell." But this is a wholly fallacious observation where the eyes are concerned because nothing from the external world impinges on the optic nerve as stimuli do upon the other organs. It is an undeniable fact that light travels at a high rate of speed, but great confusion arises when this is likened to sound.

Did you ever wonder why the eyes of a newborn infant cannot focus the eyes, although the four senses are in full working order? It is assumed that the muscles of the eyes have not yet developed sufficiently to allow this, but such is not the case. In fact, if an infant, immediately after birth, was placed in a soundproof room with its eyelids removed and kept alive for 50 years on a steady flow of intravenous glucose without allowing any stimuli to strike the other 4 organs of sense, this baby, child, young, and middle-aged person would never be able to focus the eyes to see any objects existing in that room, no matter how much light was present or how colorful they might be, simply because the conditions necessary for sight have been removed and nothing from the external world impinges on the optic nerve to cause it.

This focusing takes place for the very first time when a sufficient accumulation of sense experience (hearing, taste, touch, and smell — these are doorways in) awakens the brain, which then desires to see the source of the experience by focusing the eyes as binoculars. The eyes are the windows of the brain through which experience is gained not by what comes in but by what is looked at in relation to the afferent experience of the senses. What is seen through the eyes is an efferent experience.

Your scientists, taking for granted that five senses are an undeniable fact and becoming enthralled over the discovery that light travels at a high rate of speed, made the statement that still exists in your encyclopedias: "If we could sit on the star Rigel with a very powerful telescope focused on the Earth, we would just be able to see the ships of Columbus reaching America for the very first time." They made the assumption that since the eyes are a sense organ, it is obvious that light must reflect an electric image of everything it touches, which then travels through space and impinges on the optic nerve. But why the telescope? Let me show you where certain facts have been confused, and all the reasoning except for light traveling at a high rate of speed is completely fallacious.

THIS IS AN URGENT MESSAGE FROM A VISITOR TO YOUR PLANET

The sound from a plane, even though you can't see it, will tell you it is in the sky, but why can't you see it if an image is being reflected towards the eyes on the waves of light? An image is not being reflected. You can't see the plane simply because the distance has reduced its size to the point where it is impossible to see it with the naked eye. You can't see bacteria with the naked eye, but you can with a microscope. The reason you are able to see the moon is simply because there is enough light present and it is large enough to be seen. The reason the sun looks to be the size of the moon, although much larger, is simply because it is much farther away, as if you didn't know this, which is the reason it would look like a star to someone living on a planet trillions of miles away. This proves conclusively that the distance between someone looking, and the object seen, has no relation to time because images are not traveling towards the optic nerve on waves of light. However, this is not the same as transmitted messages that travel through space and are picked up by your ears. This means that it takes no time to see the moon, the sun, and the distant stars. In fact, if someone on Rigel had a telescope powerful enough to see a golf tournament, he would see it at the exact same time that you would, which brings up another very interesting observation.

If you couldn't see me standing right next to you because we were living in total darkness because the sun had not yet been turned on, but God was scheduled to flip the switch at noon, we would be able to see the sun instantly, at that very moment, although we would not be able to see each other for 8 minutes afterwards. The sun at noon would look exactly like a large star. To sum this up, just as you often observe that a drum corps is marching out of step to the beat when seen from a distance

29

because the sound reaches your ears after a step has been taken, likewise, if you could see someone talking on the moon via a telescope and hear his voice on the radio, you would see his lips move instantly but not hear the corresponding sound for approximately 3 seconds later. But let me prove in yet another way that the eyes are not a sense organ.

Line up 50 people who will remain motionless, and a dog, from a slight distance, cannot identify his master. If an image is traveling on the waves of light and striking the optic nerve, then he would recognize his master instantly, as he can from sound and smell. In fact, if he were vicious and trained to attack any stranger entering the back gate at night, and if his two senses — hearing and smell — were turned off, he would have no way of identifying his master and would attack, even if every part of his master's body and clothes were lit up like a Christmas tree. That is why a dog cannot identify his master from a picture or statue, which raises the question: why can man accomplish this? The answer will be given shortly.

The knowledge revealed thus far in this chapter is not what I referred to as being of significance. Frankly, it makes no difference to me that the eyes are not a sense organ, that your scientists got confused because of it, and that a dog cannot identify his master from a picture. But what does mean a great deal to me when the purpose of this book is to demonstrate how it is now possible to remove every bit of evil (hurt) from your planet is that one of the greatest forms of injustice still exists because you have never understood your true relation to the external world, which is related to what you think you see with your eyes. What is this injustice? It is to be judged an inferior production of the human race because of physiognomic differences, and this judgment takes place the moment you call one person beautiful and another ugly, handsome and homely, good-looking and bad-looking. Don't you see these differences with your very eyes? "I certainly do, but beauty is in the eyes of the beholder," which reveals your confusion even more since this expression doesn't negate the existence of beauty, it simply observes a difference of opinion as to who is considered prettier or more beautiful. You might disagree with the judges who picked Miss America, but none of the contestants would be called homely. To be classified as such is a terrible hurt, but what makes it even worse is your agreeing that other people are prettier, better looking, more beautiful or handsome than yourself, which places them in a position of superiority. But in reality, no one is beautiful or ugly, just different, and I am going to demonstrate not only how these words came into existence, but why they must come to an end out of absolute necessity. You will be given no choice in this matter because you will be compelled, by your nature, to choose that alternative for greater satisfaction.

Once it is understood as an undeniable law that nothing impinges on the optic nerve, even though the pupils dilate and contract according to the intensity of light, it becomes possible to separate what exists in the external world from that which is only a word in your head. The belief in 5 senses made it possible to imagine light waves hitting an object and reflecting an image through the eyes to the brain, for this seems logical, but how was it possible for light to reflect a value that cannot even exist in the outside world? Let me show you how this was accomplished.

As your eyes, at the age of 2 or even younger, are focused on a dog, I will repeat the word dog rapidly in your ear. When you turn away, I stop. This will be continued until you look for the dog when hearing the word, which indicates that a relation between this sound and object has been established and a photograph taken. This is obvious because even if the dog is not present when I utter the word after the relation has been formed, you would still look for the dog. This is exactly how you learn words, only I am speeding up the process.

Before long you learn the words for many things, but until you learn the word cat, you could very easily point to a cat when hearing the word dog because a photograph or negative of the difference has not yet been developed. By the same reasoning, the word Chinese takes a picture of similarities, and that is why they all look alike, as Blacks do to many people. But if you lived among them and learned their individual names, you would soon see their differences. The same thing takes place when you learn colors in a haphazard manner and are called color blind when in reality you are word blind. But when you are taught colors properly at an early age and the differences photographed in your brain, it would be impossible to be color blind unless you can't distinguish the differences before learning the words. In other words, if you can't see the difference between a fox and a dog, you would point to a fox when hearing the word dog. I believe this is clear enough, so we can move on to the next step.

Now it is extremely important to understand that a value is a personal thing. It is something you like, and although what you like exists in the external world, it is strictly a relation between you and what you like, therefore it has no existence in the world outside except for you. However, not knowing this for an absolute fact, your philosophers and lexicographers began to divide up your planet into what they considered of value by using words. Observing that more men were attracted to a certain type of woman and repelled by others, they called the one beautiful and the others ugly, homely, bad-looking, and many other names. Seeing that learning a trade and to read and write were important, educated and uneducated, intelligent and unintelligent, and a host of other words were born. This meant that from the time you were a child, your parents, relatives, and friends were expressing their likes and dislikes by using words. Over and over again, you heard, "She is so beautiful, so good-looking, so cute, so adorable, so handsome, so bad-looking, so homely, so ugly, so stupid, so uneducated," so many times, that photographs of all the differences became a permanent part of your vocabulary, and when you used or heard any of these words, you actually projected the negative of these photographs onto a screen of undeniable substance. You actually saw with your very eyes these values that existed in the external world. But let me give you an exact example of what you have been doing by using a movie projector.

Here is a screen that represents the substance of the outside world. Go up and touch it; it is real. Now I am going to drop a negative plate or slide into the projector and flip the switch. Well, just take a look; there is a picture of a girl on the screen. But when you go up to touch her, she is not there, and all you can feel is the screen itself. You have been doing the same thing with your brain projector regarding values. The differences in undeniable substance were divided up by the use of words like man, woman, child, etc., but also became a screen upon which you were able to project this value. Drop a negative plate or word slide into your brain projector and flip the switch. Well, just take a look; there is now a beautiful girl, a homely man, an ugly duckling. Turn off the switch (remove the word slide) and all you see are the differences in substance because the projected values have been removed. But since you were taught that the eyes are a sense organ that receives and transmits experiences to the brain, it was impossible to deny that this beautiful girl was a part of the real world. However, when these negatives of external value are removed, this doesn't stop you from seeing differences that appeal to you more, but instead of saying, "She is the most beautiful girl I have ever had the pleasure to meet," which places all other girls in a stratified layer of lesser value, you are compelled to say, "She appeals to me more than any girl I have ever seen," which makes it obvious that the value you see exists only for you. The first expression requires that ugly girls exist because certain types of features are considered superior, while the second expression only observes that other girls appeal to you less, which makes everybody equal in value except to you. By removing all the synonyms that describe people as good looking, nobody is hurt, but by removing all the antonyms that have been judging half the people on your planet as bad-looking, this entire group is raised to an absolute level of equality. And are you given a choice when to continue using these words after you have learned the truth only reveals your ignorance, for which you will never be blamed? And how is it possible to desire hurting people this way when you know they must excuse what you can no longer justify?

You have been compelled to look at each other through a kaleidoscope of negatives that transformed all of you realistically into what you were not. Every other word stratified external differences and similarities that could not be denied into

THIS IS AN URGENT MESSAGE FROM A VISITOR TO YOUR PLANET

external values that appeared realistic because they were seen with the direct perception of your SENSE of sight.

And now, my friends (although I know you are anxiously waiting to see how your GREAT TRANSITION can be launched, and it will be demonstrated very shortly), I will reveal knowledge that will make you very happy. In fact, I consider it the most important discovery ever made on our planet.

RUOMYES SNASSEL

CHAPTER FIVE
YOUR POSTERITY

N ow tell me, wouldn't it make you feel wonderful to know, as a matter of undeniable knowledge equivalent to two plus two equals four, that there is nothing to regret about having to die because you will be born again and again and again? I am not referring to reincarnation, to some spiritual world of souls or to any other theory, but to the flesh, to a mind and body alive and conscious of existence as you are this very moment. But before I begin, and to help you understand the proof, answer this question. Doesn't it seem strange and unbelievable that with your planet 35 billion years old (ours is 100), that you are alive at this infinitesimal fraction of time? The answer, however, can be very simply stated. The reason you are here is because your consciousness, your ability to recognize your individuality and existence, not your particular body, is the only consciousness that can ever exist. That is why you are alive at this infinitesimal fraction of time. You did with this problem, the same thing you did with free will. You inferred that since it was impossible to believe in your return after death (impossible to believe in determinism), the opposite must be true. However, let me show you once again what the perception of undeniable relations reveals.

The problem begins by not knowing that your body and consciousness are two separate entities that cannot exist one without the other, but your body is born first. It then grows and develops, and after a few years you are able to recognize your individuality and say, "I am alive, conscious of my existence." Now tell me, when you say "I," is it possible that you could be referring to someone else? Impossible, correct? This simply means that although you know other people also say "I" and are conscious of their existence, everything they say and everything in this world can only be seen through your consciousness. Proof of this is that when you talk about yourself, you don't say "he is alive," only "I am alive," and right at this point is another GREAT IMPASSE.

All through your life you say, "he died, she died, they died; he was born, she was born, they were born," and you assume that these same observations that you make during your life will continue after your death. You actually extend your reasoning beyond the grave, which is mathematically impossible to do. In other words, when you die, you can no longer say, "he is born," because this observation must pass through your consciousness, and your consciousness is no longer here since you died. So who is this child that is born? To understand who this child is, let us turn back the clock to your birth. You grow, develop, and after a few years you are able to recognize your individuality and say, "I am alive, conscious of my existence," proof of which is the fact that you are reading this book. However, you know you will eventually die. Therefore, since every child born has the innate ability to recognize the genetic differences given to him by his parents, his individuality, in other words, and since it is absolutely impossible to say "I" and be talking about someone else, one of the children born after your death can't possibly be him or her but must be you, someone who will grow, develop, recognize his individuality, and say, "I am alive, conscious of my existence." But let me clarify this in another way.

Your parents have decided to create a child. This is you but you don't know this yet. However, as luck would have it, you die during your uterine journey when your mother has a miscarriage; but still wanting you, their very own son or daughter, they try again. This time you live for one year, but die very suddenly of some unknown cause. Finally, after these heartbreaking disappointments, they have viable success and here you are. Now what is the actual difference between the you who died during your uterine journey, the "you" who died after one year, or the "you" who will die in a relatively short period of time? The difference is that in the first two cases you never became conscious of your individuality because the body that contained this potential never developed, but you died, nevertheless. In the latter case you developed your consciousness, and that is why you are able to say, "I am alive, conscious of my individuality and existence," but in reality, there is absolutely no difference because the conditions before your birth and after your death are exactly the same. Your parents have decided to create a child, and this child is YOU.

This proves conclusively that death is a mirage to those who die, and a reality only to the living; and it is your ability to understand these deeper relations that gives you your knowledge of personal immortality and your freedom from the fear of death. It is a different you who will be born again and again, but you nonetheless, not YOUR POSTERITY. However, when your loved ones die it is also true that they will never return in your lifetime because these relations are also undeniable. No one will deny that it is extremely sad to lose the people you love, but satisfaction in preserving this unliving bit of matter can only be gotten when ignorance of the truth engenders the desire. We, too, had cemeteries at one time, but now this land is used for many different things. In fact, once you understand this chapter and lose completely your fear of death, you will become a much happier and healthier individual.

The perception of these relations makes it obvious that the same general experiences you have gone through of being little boys and girls with a mother and father, growing up and remarking about the time when you believed the Earth flat, your will free, your eyes a sense organ and that you only live once, will continue just as long as you are able to reproduce yourselves.

In your new world, the inception of which will take place shortly if you are able to understand the principles in the remainder of this book, you will raise your family in complete freedom from the evils that were compelled to come into existence during your years of development. You will live to a ripe old age without ever having to worry about war and crime, and die only to be born for the same happiness again and again and again.

THIS IS AN URGENT MESSAGE FROM A VISITOR TO YOUR PLANET

PART THREE

What you have been impatiently waiting for, the knowledge of how it is now possible to launch your GREAT TRANSITION

CHAPTER SIX — YOUR NEW ECONOMIC WORLD

CHAPTER SEVEN — YOUR MEDICAL PROFESSION

CHAPTER SIX
YOUR NEW ECONOMIC WORLD

At this juncture, it is extremely important to understand that the natural law implicit in the two-sided equation cannot prevent you from finding greater satisfaction in hurting others (doing to them what they don't want done to themselves) when not to do this makes matters worse for yourself, as would be the case if you were forced, beyond your control, to lose your source of income and placed in a position where you could not meet your living expenses or acquire the necessaries of life. Just the possibility that this could happen (this pervasive insecurity) activates and justifies the law of self-preservation to lie, cheat, steal, even kill if there is no other way to get the money you need or might need for survival. Therefore, before the removal of all blame can prevent you from desiring to strike a first blow, which is to gain (to improve your standard of living) at the expense of others, it is absolutely necessary to remove the possibility that you are hurting them to prevent yourself from becoming a loser (from going below your standard of living), and there is only one way this can be accomplished.

Your standard of living is the amount of money you consume from week to week, on average, to maintain your particular way of life, but it does not include taxes, business or job expenses, insurance premiums, contributions, or any money saved, invested, or gambled with in any way that does not play an immediate role in meeting your living expenses. In other words, if your gross income is $600 per week and you suddenly lose your job or business and all your reserve cash, you might need only $3 or $400 to meet your expenses. If your gross is $1 million per week, you might only need $2000, but you alone will determine your standard of living, which will also become the basis for all your taxes. Now I am going to demonstrate (once again in an undeniable manner) that when you are guaranteed to be given the money needed should you be forced (BEYOND YOUR CONTROL) to go below your standard or to be without the necessaries of life, and then guaranteed never to be blamed no matter what you do, WAR, CRIME, AND INFLATION will come to an end out of absolute necessity, TAXES AND PRICES will be forced to come down, and your standard of living will be improved beyond your wildest expectations. To accomplish this, however, it is necessary, once again, to proceed in a step-by-step manner, and the first step is to show you that your government has been striking a first blow with impunity and in the name of justice by calling it a retaliatory blow. This occurs when you hurt others not because they did something to hurt you, but only because they did not do what you judged they should, and you blame them for their disobedience. A perfect example of this takes place when you, representing your government, fine them for going 40 miles an hour in a 25-mile zone. They did absolutely nothing to hurt anyone, but you justified taking money right out of their pockets because they violated this traffic law. This is not a criticism because it is obvious why these and similar laws came into existence, and the only reason it is mentioned is because the removal of all blame will also be unable to prevent what these laws could not. You blame people for selling drugs, their bodies, pornographic literature, and guns. You blame them for not wearing seatbelts, for taking drugs, for certain types of gambling but not others. In other words, the people selling things you don't like are simply trying to earn a living. They are completely innocent of hurting you because nothing in this world can make you swallow a drug, place a bet, buy the services of a prostitute, or do anything if you don't want to. The natural law can only prevent a first blow, and the first blow here is not what they have been doing to you, but what you have been doing to them. Let me show you how this law takes a slightly different turn to prevent you from continuing to hurt them with impunity and in the name of justice.

There exists a right of way system in human relations, as it does in the world of traffic, that also allows you to know who has the right of way when desires conflict. If you tell me what to do or what not to do, then to satisfy your desire, you need me to do something for you, but to satisfy my desire not to do what you want done, I don't require you to do anything for me. Therefore, my desire has the right of way because I am making no demands on you whatsoever. But let me elaborate a little on this.

When motor vehicle operators approach an intersection in your new world and see that the traffic light is still red, they have the right of way to do anything they want to do, but they decide to stop not because you, your government, are telling them what to do, but only because the risk of hurting you and the knowledge that they would be responsible are so terrible to contemplate when you refuse to blame them for what they cannot excuse that they are compelled to prefer stopping. But when they stop and see that it is perfectly safe to cross even though the light is still red, they have just as much of a right to do so as they had a right to cross without stopping. Though this natural law can prevent accidents because they are first blows, it can never prevent people from exceeding the recommended speed limit, from crossing on a red light, from drinking alcoholic beverages, taking drugs and driving if they think there is no risk involved to you, whereas you were hurting them only because they didn't agree with your judgment (with your laws, commandments, customs, conventions, and standards) of what was right for themselves. Therefore, the need to judge what is right for them becomes obsolete when you know they will never do anything to hurt you, which means that to criticize, blame, or hurt them in any way because they don't do what you tell them to do becomes a first blow that you cannot desire to strike when you know that they must excuse what you can no longer justify. This proves conclusively that when all people know what is a first blow you don't have to tell them not to strike it because the natural law prevents them from moving in that direction for greater satisfaction, which also means that they are completely free, their conscience clear, to do anything they judge is right for themselves without fear of criticism. For the very first time in your entire history, you will be compelled by the knowledge of your true nature, which reveals what is better for yourself, to mind your own business — that is, to stop judging what is right for others, which was impossible before.

THIS IS AN URGENT MESSAGE FROM A VISITOR TO YOUR PLANET

By blaming those not responsible, you started a chain reaction of justifiable retaliation in every walk of life, making matters a thousand times worse; but all this is coming to an end.

Now the next step is for you to estimate your standard of living and submit it to your government with a signed statement that you will never again, in return for this guarantee, ever blame anybody for anything. You will then receive a card on which will appear the amount of your guarantee, and this will allow you to get the money needed should you ever be forced into a position BEYOND YOUR CONTROL where you cannot find a job or business and do not have enough cash reserve to meet your expenses. Should an emergency arise that cannot be met with your guarantee, this will also be taken care of. However, should you quit your job, leave, or sell your business, which you certainly have the right to do if you want to, this is not beyond your control and doesn't entitle you to financial help if you are then forced to go below your standard of living, but you would still be guaranteed the basic standard. You can gamble this way if you want to, but not at the expense of the taxpayers financing the guarantee. This means that if the basic guarantee doesn't allow you to meet your expenses and the choice is either to steal from the guarantee, for which you know you would never be blamed even if the taxpayers knew what you were doing, or not to gamble with your guarantee, what choice do you have?

Once the United Nations is convinced that all of you have received your card, a day and time will be set, a holiday declared, and as it was with us many years ago, so our history recorded, you will excitedly await the countdown to launch your new world, and when zero is reached, everything locked will be unlocked, burglar alarms disconnected, floor walkers dismissed, and guards told to go home so prisoners can walk out with their card to freedom and a basic standard of living guaranteed. The armed and police forces will be displaced, along with the schools that train them and the manufacturers that equip them. There will be no need for lawmakers, judges, juries, lawyers, the Department of Motor Vehicles, liability insurance, every kind of license granting permission to do something, credit investigation and collection agencies, which include the I.R.S., all printed forms to check on your honesty, and all tax preparers. When it comes time to pay your quarterly taxes, the government accountants will announce the percent estimated, and if 10% is required and your guarantee is 300, 400, 500, 1000, 2000, 3000, etc., you would simply multiply 13 times the figure on your card and remit 10% of the total regardless of how much money you earned for that quarter. If the percent required puts you below your guarantee, you would send in what does not put you below. If any nation is unable to meet its own guarantee, the amount needed would be submitted to the United Nations, which would announce the percentage required. As you can see, there is really no further need for government, a group of people to tell you what you can and cannot do.

As a further consequence of the guarantee, labor unions will be displaced because they can only strike to gain at the expense of the taxpayers who have guaranteed to help them also in their moment of need. This also means that businesspeople will be prevented from raising prices for the same reason, which places a ceiling on everything that has a price when the transition begins, including labor. But this does not mean that an employer can't give a raise in salary or a bonus if he wants to; only that he can't use what he gives voluntarily (what might put him below his standard of living) as a justification to get financial help. As you can see, this puts an end to inflation. However, employees have the right to ask for a raise or any kind of favor, but their employer has the right of way to refuse, and if they should threaten to quit as a result of this refusal, that is their business, for which they would never be blamed, no matter how much this might hurt him. But how is it possible for them to want to quit under the changed conditions when this would only make matters worse for themselves? This does not mean that they will be denied an opportunity to improve their standard of living, only that they will be forced to do this at nobody's expense. Let me show you how this will be accomplished in our next step.

Since the displaced must use up all their reserve cash before being entitled to get financial help, billions upon billions upon billions of dollars will be drawn out of the banks, stocks, and bonds cashed in and dumped into circulation for the very first time, while all the money paid out for these displaced services will go back into the pockets of those who were paying for them. It is true that a great portion of this money will be paid out in taxes to sustain the guarantee but follow carefully what must happen.

Trillions of dollars will become available for business entrepreneurs to invest in the development of your planet (the motive will be PROFIT), WHILE MILLIONS OF THE DISPLACED WILL BE AVAILABLE FOR ON-THE-JOB TRAINING. If the gross salary on a job after training calls for $600 per week and your guarantee is 300, your employer would pay you the $300 during your training period. This would reduce the taxes needed to finance the guarantee and allow a complete on the job training program. When you have been sufficiently trained, you would then receive your gross salary and begin to pay quarterly taxes. Before long there will be such an economic boom that the amount of money needed to finance the guarantee would be reduced to an absolute minimum, which will give you that much more money to spend or invest. Furthermore, since the guarantee renders the need to save for a rainy day obsolete since you will be given the money needed should any emergency force you to go below your standard of living, that much more money will go back into your pocket because you can drop your insurance policies without hurting the insurance companies. As a further consequence, since prices cannot be raised, since there will be so much capital available, and since businesspeople will want to make as much profit as they can, they will be forced to lower prices and sell in tremendous volume, which would allow many people unable to buy something before to be able to buy it now. Instead of the vicious cycle of inflation, you will have a beneficious cycle that will benefit everyone without hurting anyone. You will soon have so many material things that the need to produce what is not being consumed will decline, causing millions of people to get laid off from their jobs. But what difference does it make when no one can get hurt? If you have things on which to spend your money that keep people employed, the taxes to finance the guarantee must come down. If you don't have anything to buy and people are laid off as a consequence, you will use this money to guarantee their standard of living. But this does not mean that you are free to spend your tax dollars, although you can if you want to. But once you fully realize that not paying your share of the taxes would be stealing from the people who would be compelled to pick up the difference but who would never blame you for this even if they knew what you were doing, how would it be possible for you to desire moving in that direction for greater satisfaction when YOU WOULD KNOW WHAT YOU ARE DOING SINCE YOU CAN NO LONGER LIE TO YOURSELF?

I don't have any more time to spare on this chapter, although you should be able to carry the economic ball from here. I would like to observe that your religious organizations get displaced but only because there is no further need for their services since God, your Creator (this world is no accident), is delivering your planet from evil. This does not mean that you have to stop going to church or synagogue if you want to, but how is it possible to want to continue spending your money in this direction when it can be used to improve your standard of living without hurting the theologians getting displaced?

It is important to clarify that NO FAULT insurance can only have reference to a hurt to yourself that you know you are responsible for. You are prevented from taking risks that could hurt others because of the changed conditions, but you are not prevented from taking risks that can only hurt yourself, and if this puts you below your standard of living and out of reach of financial help from the guarantee because the risk you chose to take was not beyond your control, you have no one to hold responsible but yourself. Therefore, you might desire to carry this kind of insurance to protect yourself against the risks you might want to take, if you can get it.

CHAPTER SEVEN
YOUR MEDICAL PROFESSION

When doctors receive their guarantee and know they will never again be blamed no matter what happens, allowing them to drop their malpractice insurance and increase their spending or investment money, they are compelled to move in a different direction for greater satisfaction. In your present world it is necessary for them to convince you that they can handle your problem, otherwise you would not employ them, and they would not get paid for their services; and that is why they produce their diplomas and a license from their government. But under the changed conditions they do not have to convince you, only themselves that they know what they are doing, and if in their professional opinion there is the slightest doubt that their treatment might make matters worse, for which they know there would be no blame, their only justification to take this risk since they can no longer be financially hurt or blamed for refusing to take on the job, is when it appears to them that you would be worse off if they prescribed nothing. For the very first time by refusing to question their qualifications or hold them responsible for your mistake in hiring them, they are compelled to hold themselves responsible unless they can convince themselves that your getting worse was not due to anything they did or didn't do. This means that if they have to choose between two risks, to prescribe something or to tell you that they really are uncertain of what to do and therefore will not take on the job, they are forced to move in the latter direction because there is no way it is possible to blame themselves for not knowing for certain what to do, whereas if you should get worse because of their advice, which implies they do know what they're doing, it becomes impossible not to blame themselves when you will never hold them responsible while guaranteeing their standard of living. This means that to prescribe medicine they would have to know all the side, distant and accumulative effects to make certain that in correcting one problem they do not create others still worse. If someone should die during surgery, the only way it is possible to clear their conscience of responsibility is to know that the patient would have died anyway had the operation not been performed, but they must convince themselves of this. They can no longer use the theory that tonsils, the appendix, and foreskin are vestigial to justify an operation unless they can also convince themselves that you are better off without these parts of your body. This will force them to become like your philosopher Socrates, who was proclaimed the wisest man of his time for discovering that one of the differences between himself and other men was that he knew he didn't know the truth about many things, whereas they didn't either but thought they did. In the majority of cases, the doctors will simply tell you, when consulted, that a drug is available that could be used for your problem, but since they cannot guarantee that it might not make matters worse because it is impossible for them to know all the side, distant, and accumulative effects, you must take whatever risks there are upon yourself. If the mother of an infant doesn't want to use her breasts for a feeding, this is her business, but she, too, will have to play doctor and select some formula because the medical profession won't. But observe another fantastic change.

Since medical students will never again need a diploma and a license to open an office and practice medicine, of what value is cheating on an examination to get what is no longer required? The only people who really have to know that they are qualified are the students themselves. Their conscience would never allow them to pretend to someone who requires their services that they are qualified, when any mistakes they make could result in a serious hurt for which they know there would be no blame. This means that a teacher will no longer be interested in finding out whether they are qualified, just as the instructor teaching you how to drive a car will not be interested in knowing whether you are qualified. This also means that asking verbal questions of students, the answers to which are already known to the teacher, makes no sense whatsoever. Asking such a question is asking them to do what they might not want to do, and since they have the right of way not to answer, the teacher is left with one alternative, that is to give them written tests along with the answers so they can mark their own papers, but this is only for their own benefit. If they are satisfied that they have learned enough, they can simply walk out of school. If they feel they haven't learned enough, they can simply stay on. In other words, there will be no more graduations and everybody becomes a dropout, sooner or later. Furthermore, although teachers have the right to recommend certain subjects to be studied, a student has the right of way to study what he wants. We have no public schools on our planet, and we do not force our children to do anything, but they read fluently at the age of five. We have no drug addicts, no alcoholics, no prostitution, and no AIDS. We like to drink at parties, just as you do, but we limit ourselves, and you know why. In the next chapter I am going to demonstrate a virtual miracle among the sexes.

THIS IS AN URGENT MESSAGE FROM A VISITOR TO YOUR PLANET

PART FOUR
The extension of this natural law into the world of love. You will also learn something about INTELLIGENCE AND EDUCATION never understood before.
CHAPTER EIGHT
PREMARITAL RELATIONS AND MARRIAGE
CHAPTER NINE
UNTIL DEATH DO THEY PART
CHAPTER TEN
PARENTS AND CHILDREN

CHAPTER EIGHT

PREMARITAL RELATIONS AND MARRIAGE

The first blow of the sexes is struck when a boy and girl are rejected by the person with whom they have fallen in love enough to desire a permanent relationship, which is marriage. More people have had their hearts broken and cut out with the knife of unrequited love than is imaginable, but I must remind you that this natural law cannot accomplish the impossible. It cannot prevent a girl or boy from rejecting the other, no matter how much the other is in love, when not to do this makes matters worse for you, as would be the case if this necessitated that you reject the person with whom you are in love or that you reject the possibility of meeting someone with whom you could fall in love as much as you are now being loved. But it can prevent your desire to take risks that get you into this kind of situation where it becomes necessary to reject the person in love, just as it prevents you from desiring to take risks that lead to automobile accidents.

To have loved and lost may be better than never to have loved at all, but this is the lesser of two evils and presupposes that there must always be a contest wherein someone loses and gets hurt, which is completely false.

Now, when a girl reaches an age where she desires to start dating (this is that time in life when the body unconsciously moves the mind in the direction of sex), she has been brought up to know that there isn't a boy alive who would desire to make her fall in love and then break her heart by leaving, because she knows that he knows that she must excuse what he can no longer justify. Consequently, when she accepts her first date with a boy who appeals to her and then finds herself falling more and more in love, whether it is returned or not (this is the key to the problem, which must be worked backwards to understand the solution), she is completely unafraid to confess her love and offer her body because she wants him for her mate and knows, just as certain as two plus two equals four, that he would never have taken her out unless the possibility existed that he could also fall in love with her. This is an undeniable fact because he knows that she would never hold him responsible for making her fall all the more in love with no intention of marrying her (staying with her permanently), or possibly making her pregnant, and when it fully dawns on him that she must excuse everything he does, although it would be his responsibility since nothing can make him hurt her this way unless he wants to, it becomes impossible for him to derive greater satisfaction from deflowering her under these conditions, unless his feelings are as genuine as hers are. This means that when a boy learns that a girl is perfectly willing to go the extreme once he has encouraged her to fall in love by kissing, petting, and fooling around in general, he recognizes there is no advantage, in fact a complete waste of time, to pay flattering compliments and hand her a line knowing that he will be compelled to refuse her body when it is offered... unless he is serious with her, that is, unless he feels, from the very first time he sees her, that he could fall in love. This forces him to ask out (the girl could ask; it makes no difference under these conditions) only the kind of girl that appeals enough to become his wife and forces her to accept her very first date with only the kind of boy that appeals enough to become her husband. They have no other choice unless they prefer the risk of making people fall in love and then find it necessary to break their hearts by leaving. But this raises the question: Suppose they discover after going together for a while that there are things about the other they don't like; are they obligated to stay? Of course not, and this was already answered. That can only happen in your world because you have hundreds of nonexisting values that are projected by words, and when you learn that your partner doesn't have some of these values or see that she is not as pretty as you would like her to be, you will keep an eye out for someone who is considered of greater value. This doesn't mean that we don't have values on our planet; only these are personal values, not something that has been projected into the external world. Should a boy be attracted to a girl with a pug, flat, or aquiline nose, small breasts, and a large rear end, he is not going to be judged because the words doing this judging have long since become obsolete. She is not homely or ugly, nor is your Miss America beautiful; they are simply different, which displaces all beauty contests. This knowledge, therefore, forces a boy and girl to search high and low for someone who has the personal values they like, someone they want to have a sexual relationship with, and they will have plenty of help to accomplish this because it is a most serious undertaking. However, if a boy should ask a girl for a date who doesn't appeal to her, she would simply turn him down as he would her, but they could not be hurt by this initial refusal. This prevents them from holding on to a string of prospects for marriage just in case they can't find someone considered of greater value, which prevents the contest wherein there must be losers who get hurt. It also means that when a boy or girl asks the other for a date, they are actually saying, in so many words, "Honey, you appeal to me very much from every point of view, and if you go out with me, I am going to accept this as an invitation, sooner or later, to make love. Consequently, when they are in a fond embrace and his hand begins to wander, instead of checking this motion as a girl was often compelled to prefer because she didn't know if this was to her advantage, she only encourages him all the more, as he encourages her. Obviously both of them will become very passionate and desire to go the extreme, but they will want this very much without the slightest fear, and the very moment they indulge with or without contraception, regardless of what they do to satisfy each other, they become, believe it or not, husband and wife, but only because they will fall so much in love when nothing inhibits their sexual pleasure and they are prevented from striking a first blow, that they will never desire another sexual partner. Now tell me, in this kind of world where boys and girls get married very young, and then live happily ever after, can prostitution develop or continue to exist? Is it possible for them to desire any kind of adulterous relation, ANY KIND, when they are so satisfied with their partner that just the thought never enters their mind? Even masturbation, and there is nothing wrong with this because it hurts nobody, is not preferred when their primary desire is to satisfy each other. Many things end under the changed conditions. Are they too young to get married?

God created them with a built-in standard as to when they are ready to enjoy a complete sexual relationship which has nothing to do with when they will feel ready to raise a family. This will compel them to be very careful and think like never before, because they won't want to burden their parents or the taxpayers with additional expenses when they know there will be no blame. But the enjoyment of a sexual relationship after learning how to satisfy each other to the fullest (which will make them fall more and more in love) wouldn't cost their parents or the taxpayers a dime. They will remain together, as you will soon have verified, not only because to leave would break the other's heart, who would never blame them for this, but primarily because it would break their own heart.

In your present world, you can get married without having sexual intercourse and have the latter without the former, but in your new world, it will be impossible to have one without the other because they are one and the same. And this will apply to men and women of all ages.

Boys and girls never gave much thought to the consequences of their actions because they were driven by a natural desire for sex, and when somebody fell in love and got hurt, the answer was, "What was I supposed to do, marry the girl because she got pregnant? She knew what she was doing by not using protection, and I didn't commit myself." Knowing that he would be blamed, he was always allowed to shift his responsibility, but he had no better choice because the pressure for a sexual relationship was striking the first blow since marriage was out of the question at that young age. By removing all the blame, the pressure is also removed because he can have sexual intercourse immediately, and there is no possibility for unrequited love to develop, no chance for a girl to lose her virginity out of wedlock, no chance for a double standard to make some girls bad and others good, and no chance for a boy and girl to hurt each other in any way where sex is concerned because all the factors truly responsible are prevented from arising. Furthermore, once all the words are removed that judge many people as inferior physiognomic productions of the human race, everybody becomes perfectly equal in value except for the person making a choice. One face is not better looking than another; it is just different, although you will always find certain differences you like better. It is true that you have already been conditioned to move in the direction of certain differences, but you cannot be hurt when these differences reject you at the very outset and when other differences will never again be directly or indirectly criticized, which in your present world could possibly make you regret your choice and keep an eye out for someone who would be looked upon by others as having more to offer in the way of physical appearance. But how is it possible for you to regret your preference for a mate when you have fallen in love, which takes place after, not before, sexual intercourse?

In your present world, the meaning of love after marriage takes place is a horse of another color, for the intensity of your desire to continue loving the other depends solely on the degree of sexual satisfaction, which proves conclusively that the stronger the passion, the greater will this feeling be of love and devotion, and further demonstrates why there is so much adultery on your planet. Most couples remain together after physical satisfaction has sunk to its lowest ebb, not because they are still in love (desire a sexual relationship with each other except as a last resort or to fulfill an obligation), but only because it is the lesser of two evils when divorce is considered worse. But observe, in the next chapter, another virtual miracle.

RUOMYES SNASSEL

CHAPTER NINE
UNTIL DEATH DO THEY PART

The problem in your present marriages begins with you not knowing who has the right of way when desires conflict, which allows you to use fallacious standards to judge what your partners should do for you. You justified criticizing them for wanting to sleep alone by invoking sleeping together as a condition of marriage. You expected them to show their love by sacrificing their desire in favor of yours, which only reveals your selfishness because their desire doesn't require you to do anything, whereas your desire plainly tells them not to go to another room or bed. There is nothing wrong with desiring to sleep together, but it cannot be satisfied unless they want the same thing. Then, when they still insisted on sleeping alone (insisted on doing many things you didn't like or approve of), and because you believed you were right, you called them selfish and struck a first blow to get even, which started a chain reaction of resentment. But when you know they have the right of way to do anything they want to do and that they would never blame you for criticizing and hurting them for not satisfying your desire, you are given no choice but to sacrifice your selfishness and respect desires that make no demands on you.

With sexual intercourse, you have a slightly different problem (and here is where most of the trouble begins) because this is something you cannot do alone, yet to tell your partners that you are in the mood and expect them to honor your desire or to touch them in any way for that purpose takes for granted that they also want to make love or be fondled at that moment. Since this, too, is an act of selfishness because it is a judgment of what you expect them to do for you unless they also desire this relationship, you cannot touch them for that purpose until they extend an invitation. This means that since you cannot make any physical contact because you do not know if this is what they want, you have no choice but to do everything in your power, one way or another, to arouse their desire to accept your invitation without touching them in any way, which then gives them the right to make physical contact with you if they want to. This means that you must do everything possible to prevent their lack of desire, but almost 100% of the time, because there will be no arguments or criticism, they will be sufficiently aroused to accept your invitation.

The expression "for better or for worse" in your world, allows you to strike a first blow, making it worse for your partners, and then excuse it by saying, "You married me for better or for worse." This permits you to get out of that shape that originally attracted them, and then when their desire diminishes because you are less appealing, you blame them for what is your responsibility. But in your new world, knowing they will never blame you for letting yourself get out of that shape that originally attracted them, you are forced to do everything in your power to make their sexual life better because they will never hold you responsible for making it worse. The very fact that you are prevented from taking your partners for granted and must arouse their desire to accept an invitation each and every time you are in the mood, will cause the greatest amount of passion imaginable. The honeymoon will never be over because you will keep yourself fit as a fiddle and ready for love.

Now, a great source of arguments arises when you try to save yourself physical effort by getting them to do for you what you are fully capable of doing for yourself. This occurs when you ask them to do you a favor, which is a euphemistic way of telling them what to do because you get angry when they refuse. But when you know that they have the right of way to refuse what you have the right to ask, you will never ask favors of each other except in rare cases, which will compel them to ask if there is anything they can do for you and then not to take advantage of this generous offer because to do so would reveal your selfishness, not your love, you are forced to restrict your requests only to those things you know would be a pleasure for them to do for you.

When your transition gets launched, all the laws regarding marriage and divorce will become obsolete, which means that you are free to leave your partners if it can give you greater satisfaction. But if you have been supporting your family and decide to walk away from this obligation, you will force them to get financial assistance from the guarantee to help meet their standard of living, which literally means that you would be stealing money from the taxpayers who would never blame you even if they knew. BUT YOU WOULD KNOW, and this would never give you greater satisfaction. This does not mean that you can't continue having adulterous relations if you want to, but when you fully realize that your partners will never blame you for this or anything you choose to do and will remove all the first blows they have been striking, you will be forced to move in an entirely different direction for your happiness. Instead of running away when given the freedom to do so, you will decide to remain, and then when all the causes of your arguments have been removed and you begin to respect each other's desires, who knows, you might even extend an invitation to make love. But remember, your NEW WORLD must become a reality sooner or later. How long it will take is up to you.

I will conclude this book by touching briefly on children and education.

CHAPTER TEN
PARENTS AND CHILDREN

The next and final hurt to be removed is what you have been doing to your children. However, this occurs only when you use fallacious standards to justify criticizing and punishing them for doing and not doing that for which they have the right of way. You blame them for disliking the food you want them to eat and for liking what you don't want to be eaten. You are blamed by society, and then you blame them for not having good manners, for not dressing properly, for not going to bed at the proper time, for not getting good grades, and for a hundred other things. They are blamed and punished so much that it is no wonder they react with such hostility. Not only that, but they are put down so much because they are not considered pretty or bright, perhaps even ugly or stupid, that it is no wonder they developed such an inferiority complex that many of them preferred suicide for greater satisfaction. However, once you understand that they have the right of way to do anything they desire, just so they are not hurting others or themselves, you are given no choice but to remove all the fallacious standards by which they have been judged. But remember, you had no choice to be otherwise in your present environment because you wanted to avoid the criticism of others. But when your transition is officially launched, the pressure put on you by society will be permanently removed, and just observe what must come to pass.

If you want them to eat certain food, you must prepare it in such a way that they will like it because you can no longer blame them, as you now do with threats of punishment, for not liking it. If you want them to be in bed at a certain time, and they don't agree with you, they have the right of way, which means that if this is that important to you and you have to sacrifice watching a television show so they will imitate your going early to bed, what choice do you have? On our planet, they go to bed when they're tired. They simply say, "Good night; I'm going to bed." If they see us taking a drink, and want to taste it, we never deny them, and rarely, if ever, do they like what they taste. In fact, they wonder what there is that we like. But if you are worried that this might turn them into an alcoholic, don't drink in front of them or do anything you don't want them to imitate. However, if any of their desires require that you do something you don't want to do, for whatever reason, YOU HAVE THE RIGHT OF WAY and must not give in unless what they want is not a possible hurt to others or themselves and is not a burden to you. If this is explained properly, they will understand, but if they don't, you must never give in, and they will very soon know what they can and cannot expect from you and will never ever become spoiled. Now let us turn to something much more serious.

It is demanded by your conscience, once the principles in this book are thoroughly understood, that you treat every person on your planet with equal respect, but this is denied by words that make certain people superior productions of the human race. You now understand, or at least I think you do, that no one is beautiful or ugly, just different, but who will believe that no one is educated or uneducated, intelligent or unintelligent? However, before you jump to any premature conclusions, let me explain certain facts.

Bearing in mind that nothing of value can exist in the external world except in relation to you, the word intelligent is used to symbolize the favorable result of an I.Q. test, and when some people tested are unable to do as well as others, they are called less intelligent or unintelligent. But in reality, the only thing you really know when the word intelligent is removed is that some people can do certain things better than others, which is an undeniable fact.

Supposing you used the ability to play chess as a test to determine the I.Q. of your professors and then graded them as to how well they did against the champion of the world. Wouldn't you call most of them unintelligent in comparison? Can't you see now, once the word intelligent is removed, that the most you can say is that these professors are inferior chess players, which is an undeniable fact, but that doesn't make them unintelligent. By symbolizing the different results in an I.Q. test with words like very intelligent, brilliant, a genius, you developed the other words like not so intelligent, stupid, very stupid, and then you projected these nonexisting values onto a screen of undeniable differences, which were then seen with your very eyes. Can't you see that some people are unintelligent, some stupid, and others very intelligent? These word slides in your brain projector allow you to raise the opinion of yourself by putting others down. You will understand this much better with regard to the word education. Here is a word that has confused the most developed minds because it implies that the more education you acquire, the more educated and valuable you become, which means that those who do not partake of it will be judged uneducated and of lesser value. If you decide to drop out of school, you are not as educated as the individual who graduates high school, who is less educated than the college dropout, who is less educated than the Ph.D., who is less educated than certain professors. As a consequence of this external value, which is seen with your eyes, you are treated with greater respect the more of it you acquire. Certain diplomas exact the title of doctor, which requires that the people who earned this honor look down on you with less respect than is shown to them, and someone who never learned to read and write is made to feel as if he is a nonentity in the presence of these educated giants. But Will Durant, whose Story of Civilization I had the privilege of reading, resented the preemption of education by the colleges and defined it in a way to include those who did not finish school but continued to read and study on their own, which made the universities dislike him while the dropouts loved him. To him, education was a definite reality, something of great value, but he didn't know he was dealing only in words. It is absolutely true that someone who has learned certain things will prove more valuable to a corporation that requires this knowledge, just as certain features will prove more valuable to a movie studio, but this doesn't make either one of greater intrinsic value. If you desire to read 10,000 books and go to school for 30 years, this is your business, but it does not make you any more educated than a particular physiognomy will make you handsome. You are actually different than the person who never went to school, never read a book, and fished for 30 years, but this does not entitle you to more respect, which is what takes place when the word educated projects this value. Removing all the synonyms and antonyms of the words intelligent and educated doesn't mean that children will lose their desire to learn, because what they prefer to do with their time is conditioned by what they want to become, but it does mean that they will never again be shown less respect no matter what they look like or what they desire, or do not desire, to study.

In reality, you are acquiring an education from the day of your birth to the day of your death, which renders that word as useful as the words human and mankind. All of you are members of the human race and part of the MANKIND SYSTEM, and all of you have acquired an education. In concluding this rather brief work, and to show you what words can do in a more concrete fashion, I am going to quote Will Durant on education and then paraphrase his thought.

He writes, "I believe that it is through reading, rather than high school and college, that we at last acquire a liberal education. Today we think a man is educated if he can read the newspapers morning, noon and night; but though our colleges turn out graduates like so many standardized Fords every year, there is a visible dearth of real culture in our life; we are a nation with a hundred thousand schools, and hardly a dozen educated men. Education should make a man complete; it should develop every creative power in him, and open his mind to all the enjoyable and instructive aspects of the world. A man who is heavy with millions, but to whom Beethoven or Corot or Hardy, or the glow of the autumn woods in the setting sun, is only sound and color signifying nothing, is merely the raw material of a man; half the world is closed to the blurred windows of his spirit.

Education does not mean that we have become certified experts in business, or mining, or botany, or journalism, or epistemology; it means that through the absorption of the moral, intellectual and esthetic inheritance of our race we have come to understand and control ourselves as well as the external world; that we have chosen the best as our associates both in spirit and in the flesh; that we have learned to add courtesy to culture, wisdom to knowledge, and forgiveness to understanding. When will our colleges produce such men?"

However, this may be from his point of view, from his effort to define a word that in your new world will apply equally to everyone (and this paraphrase is not in any way a criticism of Will Durant), "we are able to control and understand ourselves as well as the external world," not because you have absorbed the "moral, intellectual, and esthetic inheritance of our race," but only because you know what it means that your eyes are not a sense organ, that your will is not free, and why there is nothing to fear in your own death. "We have chosen the best as our associates both in spirit and in the flesh," only because the knowledge that you will never be criticized or ridiculed allows you, for the very first time, to select what is truly best for yourself, even though you may prefer the Beetles to Beethoven, Zane Grey to Shakespeare, Elvis Presley to Caruso, the atmosphere of a pool hall to the "glow of the autumn woods in the setting sun," or a garbage collector for a friend to an author, philosophical historian, or piano virtuoso. "We have learned to add courtesy to culture, and wisdom to knowledge," only because you have learned to mind your own business, learned what respect is, learned that all mankind are perfectly equal in intrinsic value, and learned how unconsciously ignorant of the truth you have always been, which wisdom makes it impossible to be discourteous when there is no culture, no education, no beauty, and no other words to make you feel that you are an inferior production of the human race. And you have added "forgiveness to understanding," only because you know at last that man is truly not to blame, which gives you the understanding to prevent from coming back that for which forgiveness was previously necessary. "When will our colleges produce such men?" Never in your present world, and only when your political leaders understand the principles and make plans to launch your GREAT TRANSITION.

And now, my friends, it is time for me to say goodbye. But remember, no matter how long it takes for this to begin, YOU WILL BE THERE.

Dear Reader:

If you found this message compelling and would like to learn more, you can go to:

http://www.declineandfallofallevil.com

You can also visit us on our Facebook page at:

www.facebook.com/determinismandconscience[1]

It is our hope that you will give this book a positive review as it will help to get this knowledge formally investigated. With enough people on board doing whatever they can to pass this knowledge along, we may not have to wait 500 years for this discovery to be brought to light but may actually get to witness the Great Transition in our very own lifetime.

Thank you.

---

1.   http://www.facebook.com/determinismandconscience

Did you love *This Is An Urgent Message From A Visitor To Your Planet*? Then you should read *Decline and Fall of All Evil*[2] by Seymour Lessans!

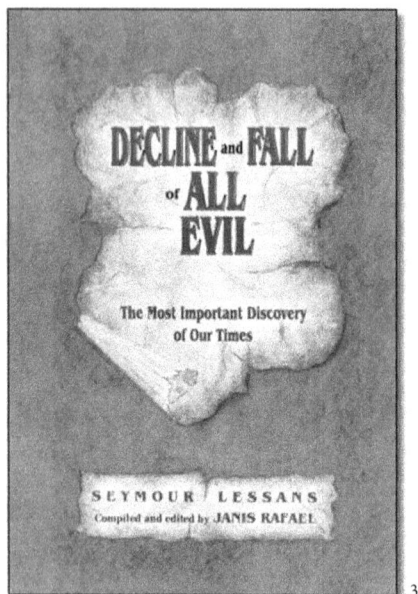

Many theories as to how world peace could be achieved have been proposed, yet war has once again taken its deadly toll in the 21st century. The dream of peace has remained an unattainable goal — until now. The following pages reveal a scientific discovery regarding a psychological law of man's nature never before understood. This finding was hidden so successfully behind layers and layers of dogma and misunderstanding that no one knew a deeper truth existed. Once this natural law becomes

2. https://books2read.com/u/bppd0X

3. https://books2read.com/u/bppd0X

a permanent condition of the environment, it will allow mankind, for the very first time, to veer in a different direction — preventing the never-ending cycle of hurt and retaliation in human relations. Although this discovery was borne out of philosophical thought, it is factual, not theoretical, in nature.

Read more at www.declineandfallofallevil.com.

www.ingramcontent.com/pod-product-compliance
Lightning Source LLC
Chambersburg PA
CBHW050548280326
41933CB00011B/1763